HOW TO BEAD

French Embroidery Beading

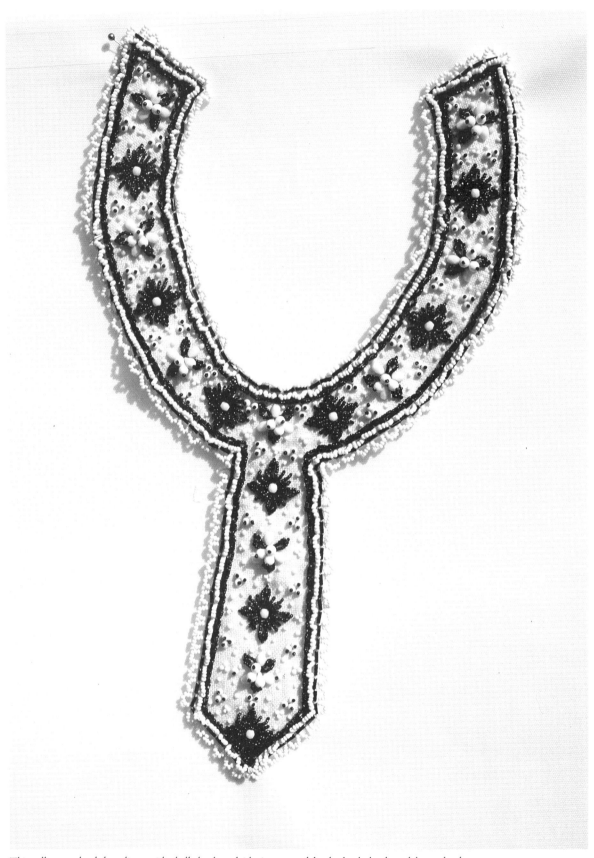

This collar was beaded on linen with chalk beads and 'shot' navy seed beads; bugle beads and larger beads were added for the centre; chalk beads in loops of seven form the edge finish

HOW TO BEAD

French Embroidery Beading

Maisie Jarratt

Kangaroo Press

Acknowledgments

My thanks to those who have helped in the creation of this book—for
photography, Tim Wade of Nowra; for typing, Debra Moore of
Gerringong; and for overall support, my husband G. Duncan Jarratt.

First published in Australia in 1991 by Kangaroo Press
an imprint of Simon & Schuster (Australia) Pty Limited
20 Barcoo Street, East Roseville NSW 2069

A Viacom Company
Sydney New York London Toronto Tokyo Singapore

Printed in Hong Kong through Colorcraft Ltd

10 9 8 7

Contents

Introduction

Beading as a form of fabric decoration has been around for a very long time. Unfortunately few early examples survive, only the beads themselves lasting longer than the background fabric or the thread that fixed them to it.

Most recently, in Victorian times beading enjoyed great popularity among ladies of leisure. After World War I the use of beading as clothes decoration, combined with fringing and bows, really took off in the heady atmosphere of the 1920s. Since then beading has always been with us, its popularity changing with changing fashions.

Beading has generally been used to decorate and embellish clothing, mainly women's fashion frocks and gowns, which were adorned with beads, sequins, stones, pearls and braid. As fashions change, so do beading designs. Over the years the methods of manufacture of beads and sequins have also changed.

There are two types of beading—hand beading and French frame beading, also known as tambour.

In hand beading, designs are made by sewing the beads onto the fabric one by one with a fine bead needle, using machine thread. I was taught this art by Mademoiselle Bon in a French workroom where exclusive gowns were designed and made. I have been embroidery beading for the past fifty-four years, being in my early teens when I started.

In French frame beading, the material is attached to a frame and the beads are 'worked' on. This technique was introduced to Australia in the mid-1920s by Madame Lorrémo of France, who taught this exclusive art to me and many others. The method is quite involved and is fully explained later.

By writing this book on embroidery beading and design I am endeavouring to pass on my knowledge of this fascinating and lovely art. Like my teachers I have taught many girls and women in my lifetime, and continue to do so.

Maisie Jarratt

A brief history

The 1920s

Evening top, 1920s

This heavily beaded garment was worked in France in the 1920s. It is an example of French frame beading, also known as tambour beading. At that time, pure silk chiffon was the fabric most frequently used.

The 1930s

This 'crazy' pattern was a very popular form in frame beading in the 1930s. It was usually used to decorate full length gowns. This type of flat beading was the principal method of working in the 1930s. The section on frame beading (page 43) gives several more examples of this kind of work.

'Crazy' beading

The 1960s

The heavily beaded handworked collar shown in Plate 1 inside the front cover is an example of the crusty method of embroidery popular in the 1960s.

During this period I designed and embroidered lace bras for the Berlei company. The bra was encrusted with beads, sequins, crystals and stones and worn under a sheer blouse. This photograph shows one of them. Recently beaded bras have become popular again; one appears in the second photograph.

Lace bra from the 1960s

Lace bra, 1990

Beading and design

Beading and designing requires a creative approach, so let your imagination run free.

I always keep a lookout for objects that would look decorative as beadwork. Flowers are good subjects, as there are so many different petals and centres. Butterflies are also good; you can blend many different coloured sequin combinations to give a varying number of looks. See Plate 2 inside the front cover.

I have included many designs that are very easy to bead. To enhance a simple design, remember that trailing leaves, scrolls and spotting can always be used. Designs can be taken from jewellery, from abstract patterns and especially from fabrics.

Once you have learned to bead and have enough confidence to start working on a jumper, blouse or frock, with pencil and tracing paper try jotting down some designs. Don't get too elaborate to begin with—a little practice might also be a good idea.

A lot of patience is essential in the beginning, but if you like handwork, beading is very easily learned. It is very relaxing to sit and bead and very rewarding once you have achieved your goal.

Starting a garment, always choose a soft material which you are sure you can work. Jersey is very good but *do not stretch it* when beading. Coordinate the bead colours with the fabric.

Buy only a few beads and sequins to start with; you will soon add to your collection as you build up the colours you will need for different items. The range of beads, sequins, stones and crystals can be bewildering. Buy some wooden beads, some chunky beads and large bold sequins to coordinate with the colours you already have; these will be useful when you come to work on thick heavy knits or heavy material. By contrast, delicate fabrics such as sheer (or georgette) and lace need tiny seed beads.

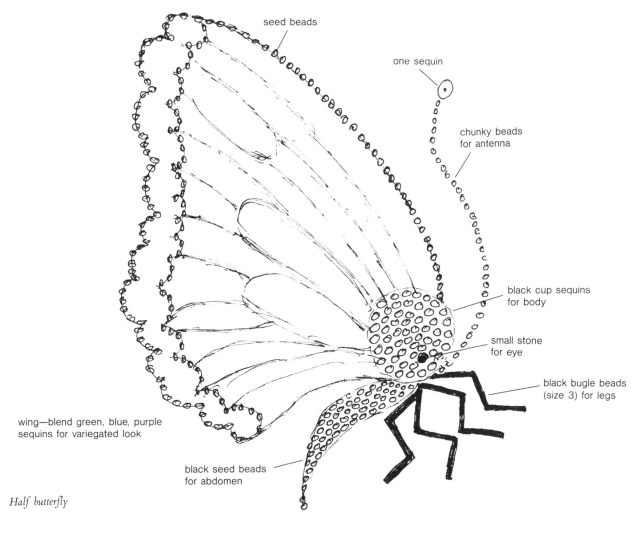

seed beads

one sequin

chunky beads for antenna

black cup sequins for body

small stone for eye

black bugle beads (size 3) for legs

wing—blend green, blue, purple sequins for variegated look

black seed beads for abdomen

Half butterfly

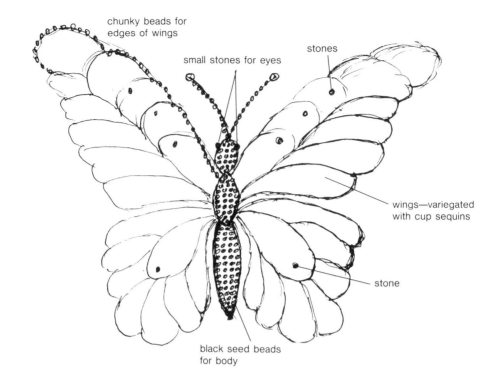

chunky beads for
edges of wings

small stones for eyes

stones

wings—variegated
with cup sequins

stone

Butterfly

black seed beads
for body

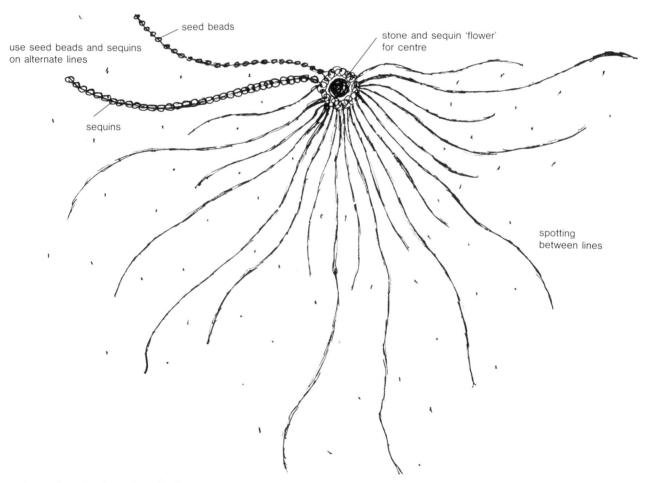

seed beads

stone and sequin 'flower'
for centre

use seed beads and sequins
on alternate lines

sequins

spotting
between lines

Abstract design based on a butterfly shape

Equipment

Fabric of any texture can be embroidered with beads, sequins, pearls and stones. You may embroider an already completed article, or a piece of fabric which will later be made up into a bag or collar.

The equipment you will need includes:

1. Fine bead needles (sharps or straws), Nos. 11 and 12, are most commonly used. Some beads have such very small holes that a much finer needle may be required.
2. Polyester machine threads. Always use a colour that matches the colour of the fabric being embroidered.
3. Tracing paper and a fade-away pencil to draw designs onto fabric.
4. A piece of felt or cotton sheeting to lay on the work table. This not only provides a place for the beads to rest but makes picking them up much easier. Hint: It makes life easier to spread out just a few beads at the one time.
   or
   A flat tray covered with a piece of felt or cloth is ideal on which to place the beads and work from. It allows you to embroider without disturbing the beads and is most convenient if you have to move your work.
5. Needle holders, whose use is described later (page 43) are an important piece of equipment for crusted beading.

All these things are illustrated in colour on page 17.

Embroidery beads

There are many different types of beads, including seed, chunky, bugle, two-cut, three-cut and round moulded. They may be made of crystal, glass, ceramic, wood—even plastic. Each type comes in many sizes and colours, e.g. bugle beads are obtained in Sizes 1, 2 and 3, and also come in an extra long form. The most expensive beads are the three-cut beads.

After you have been embroidering with beads for a while you will be amazed at how many different types of bead are available, and just how many of them you have in your own collection.

Sequins

Sequins come in two types—cup shaped and flat—and in a bewildering variety of colours and sizes to match any bead in your collection. Gold, silver and crystal sequins used with contrasting beads add a very decorative note to almost any design.

Stones

Rhinestones and crystal drops of all sizes are available to blend in with most beads and sequins.

Pearls

Pearls add to the lustre of a piece of embroidery. They range from tiny seed pearls to quite large sizes, and come in a variety of shades. Pearl drops, which are white and cream, are available in many shapes and sizes; they are frequently used with crystal beads on wedding gowns and head-dresses.

Methods

Tracing a design

1. Having chosen the design you wish to embroider sketch it out on tracing paper with firm, bold lines, and transfer it to the fabric, using one of the new fade-away pencils designed for this very purpose.

2. It is a good idea to run a tacking thread around the design. Sometimes the pencil fades away while you are working the design and the thread saves a lot of retracing. The thread can be pulled out when the beading is completed.

3. Collect together the different beads and sequins needed for the design, and lay them out on the felt workcloth.

4. If you are uncertain of your bead choices, sew a few beads and sequins onto a small sample of the fabric to see how they suit the design and the material.

Washing Instructions

1. *Hand wash* in cold water with Softly or a wool wash.
2. Rinse, and *drip dry* in the shade.
3. Iron on the *wrong side* of the garment with the beading resting on a towel—press on a warm iron setting only.
4. *DO NOT* wash in a machine or tumble dry.

Important

1. The flow of the work is in general from right to left, and *always* towards you. Left handed people will work in the opposite direction, but the principles remain the same.

2. Always use *double-threaded cotton*, knotted at the end, when sewing on beads, sequins and stones.

3. Wherever the type of stitch to be used has not been stipulated, use a *whip stitch*, sewing in a right to left movement.
   Bugle beads are usually sewn with a *back stitch*, but whip stitch is also used in some designs.

4. Always stitch the large central bead of a flower spray *twice* to ensure its hold on the material.

5. Your intended method of beading should be *practised* on a sample of the fabric you will be working on *before* you begin.

6. Treat the fabric you are working gently, and *do not stretch it*. This especially applies to jersey. Stretched material bounces back when tension is released and puckers up the beadwork.

7. As with all sewing, *wash your hands* before you start.

Seed beads

Sewn one at a time

1. Spread seed beads out on the cloth or tray.
2. Draw a straight line on the fabric with a fade-away pencil as a guide to bead on.
3. Thread 1 bead and sew to fabric with a whip stitch, moving from right to left below the bead.
4. Thread another bead and sew it in the same manner.
5. Continue sewing beads, ensuring that they are evenly spaced, as they will look cluttered if sewn too closely.
6. When your straight lines look even and balanced try a gentle curve. See the photograph on the next page.

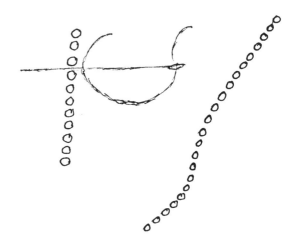

Sewing seed beads one at a time

Sewn three at a time

This is a quick method of sewing when working scrolls, particularly those which have a number of tight curves.
1. Thread 3 beads to the needle and sew them with a whip stitch on a downwards angle (i.e. sew towards yourself), ensuring that the beads lie flat on the fabric.
2. Thread a further 3 beads and sew in the same manner. Continue until the required length is sewn. .

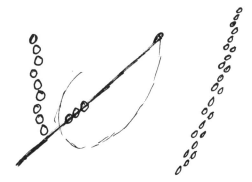

Sewing seed beads three at a time

Bugle beads

Sewn one at a time

This method of sewing bugle beads uses back stitch. Remember to always sew *towards* yourself, not away.
1. Spread bugle beads out on cloth.
2. With a fade-away pencil draw the design to be embroidered.
3. Start by bringing the needle up through the fabric one bugle-bead length away from the starting point.
4. Thread 1 bugle bead and sew on with a back stitch, bringing the needle up again at a point half the length of the bugle bead away from the starting point.
5. The beads lie at an angle, half overlapping, as the illustration demonstrates.
6. Repeat from Step 3.

Sewing bugle beads one at a time

Half bugle beads (size 2)

Sewn around a curve

Sewing bugle beads around a curve can be difficult as the beads have to be angled to work around the curve. This is effected by sewing the beads closely together on the inside of the curve with their outer ends spaced slightly further apart. This technique is worth practising many times over.

Sewing bugle beads (size 2) around a curve

Curves embroidered in seed beads and bugle beads

Sequins

Sewn one at a time

The thread used for sewing sequins must match the colour of the sequins. For sewing gold or silver sequins use a gold or silver metallic thread.

Method

1. Draw a straight line with a fade-away pencil for practising.
2. Spread sequins onto cloth.
3. Thread 1 sequin and sew to material with a whip stitch, moving right to left.
4. Thread another sequin, insert the needle into the fabric just under the bottom edge of the first sequin sewn and sew the whip stitch.
5. Continue sewing in this manner until the required length has been sewn. Each new sequin will slip under the previous sequin up to the centre hole, thereby covering each holding thread.
6. This technique needs practising to get an even appearance. When a straight line looks good, practise some curves.

Remember

- Keep the sequins evenly spaced.
- Sew right to left.
- Sew cup sequins with the cup side *up*.

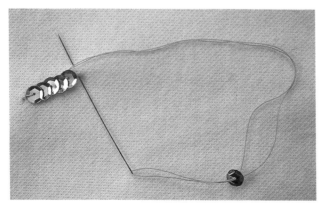

Sequins sewn one at a time

Seed beads and cup sequins

Method 1

1. Thread 3 seed beads and 1 cup sequin together, ensuring that the sequin is cup side up.
2. Using a whip stitch, sew from right to left, keeping the beads and sequin flat on the material so they do not bunch up. The 3 beads should fit neatly into the cup of the sequin.
3. The next 3 beads and sequin should just fit under half of the first sequin.

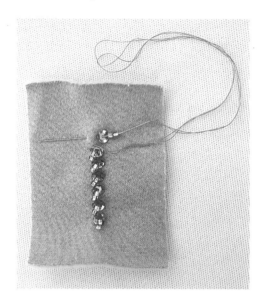

Method 2

1. Thread 3 seed beads together and sew in a straight line, using a whip stitch. These beads should lie flat on the material.
2. Bring needle up at the third bead and thread another 3 beads and 1 sequin. Sew these on an outwards angle.
3. Return thread neatly under the fabric, and sew another 3 beads and 1 sequin on an angle to the other side of the line.
4. Return neatly under fabric and repeat from Step 1, angling outwards on every third bead.

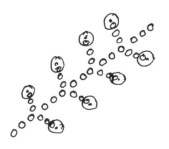

Bugle beads and seed beads

Method

1. Thread and sew bugle beads individually along a line, using a whip stitch as a spacer between the beads. Remember to sew right to left.
2. Return to the first whip stitch space, thread together 4 seed beads and sew across between the bugle beads.
3. Continue sewing seed beads between each bugle bead in a straight line.

Bugle beads and chunky beads

Method

1. Sew on a size 3 bugle bead with a whip stitch, moving right to left.
2. Sew 1 chunky bead in the same manner.
3. Repeat. These beads can form angles of different degrees which can be used on any part of a design. This is the French method of sewing on beads, which can be used in many ways, as the illustrations demonstrate.

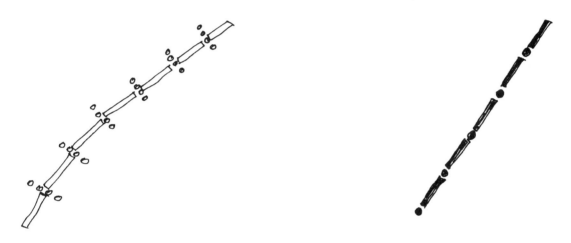

One way of using bugle beads and chunky beads to make a simple flower design more interesting

Bugle beads, seed beads and cup sequins

Method 1

1. Sew 1 bugle bead, using a whip stitch.
2. Thread 3 seed beads and 1 cup sequin together. Using a whip stitch, moving right to left, sew them below the bugle bead.

This technique can be used on the large coloured flower shown in Plate 16, or wherever it is appropriate in a design.

Method 2

1. Thread together 3 seed beads and 1 sequin and sew on with a whip stitch. Repeat.
2. When the required length is embroidered, take size 3 bugle beads one at a time and sew them at an angle on each side of the sequin. Keep returning the thread neatly under the fabric—do not cut until the end.

 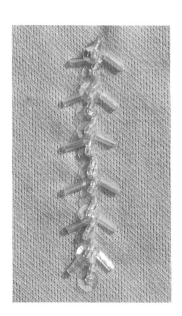

Wooden beads, chunky beads and cup sequins

Wooden beads can be obtained in many colours as well as various natural shades. There are multitudes of shapes and sizes—round, square, oblong, oval. The oval shape is perfect for flower work.

Method

1. Draw a curved line as the basis for a flower spray.
2. Sew 1 oval shaped wooden bead onto the line with a whip stitch.
3. Sew on 1 chunky bead, then a further wooden bead, continuing in this manner until the 'spray' is the required length.
4. Working outwards from a chunky bead, thread a further 2 chunky beads, 1 small cup sequin, 1 bead and 1 large sequin together. Sew this combination on alternate sides of every second chunky bead.

Brown wooden beads with gold and black sequins are very smart! See Plate 9. In general, wooden beads look best used on linen, wool or coarse lace.

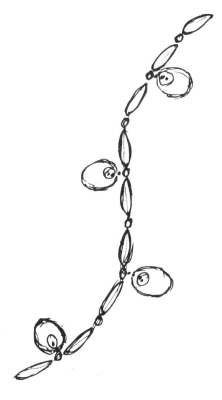

A simple curved flower spray based on wooden beads and cup sequins

Plates 5 and 6   *The equipment you will need—see page 11*

Plate 7 (below)   *Bugle beads sewn with a single chunky bead between, with chunky beads and a single sequin, and in an elaborately angled pattern—see pages 15 and 16*

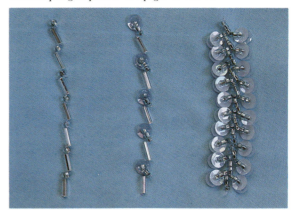

Plate 8   *A large elaborate flower motif using a number of techniques—page 23*

Plate 9 (right)   *An arrangement of wooden beads, chunky beads and cup sequins (page 16), and a wooden bead flower described on page 21*

Plate 10 *A scroll design featuring split leaves and teardrops (page 34)*

Plate 11 *A scroll with a sequin flower (page 35)*

Plate 12 *Elaborate motifs described on page 37*

Plate 13 *(right)   This simple zig-zag pattern (page 38) looks much more difficult than it is*

Plate 14 This design is based on a pattern given on page 24

Plate 15 (right) Many are the variations that can be worked from a paisley outline

Plate 17 (below) An example of beaded guipure lace flowers (page 41)

Plate 16 Unworked cabbage roses and an embroidered hibiscus flower (page 25)

Plate 18 (left) One of many possible variations of a scroll pattern

19

Plate 19 *A collection of dolls with beaded gowns*

Plate 20 *Double looped beaded fringing (page 40)*

Plate 21 *Lampshade decorated with double looped fringing in various shades of blue*

Plate 22 *(top right) This doll's lace dress is a copy of an adult gown (page 41)*

Plate 23 *(bottom right) An elaborately embroidered snake combining all the flatwork methods outlined in this book (page 41)*

Designs

Wooden bead flower

You will need

Size 3 bugle beads
Round yellow wooden bead
5 oval shaped natural wooden beads
20 green chunky beads, plus
10 chunky beads

Method

1. Sew bugle beads on an angle along a curve, one at a time, using back stitches, to form the flower stem. Leave a 3-bead space for the flower.
2. Sew the yellow wooden bead in the centre of the space, sewing twice to secure.
3. Sew the 5 oval shaped wooden beads in position to form the flower petals.
4. Thread together 4 green chunky beads and sew outwards between the wooden bead petals. Repeat in each petal space.
5. Down the stem below the flower, position in place and sew outwards from the stem 5 chunky beads, threaded together, to form a leaf. Repeat on the other side of the stem.

Several flowers can easily be combined to form a spray.
A colour photograph of this design appears on page 19.

Medium sized bead and sequin flower

You will need

Cup sequins
Seed beads
Pearl or glass bead

Method

1. Secure the pearl or glass bead to the material to form the centre of the flower.
2. Bring the needle up beside the centre bead and thread together 3 beads, 1 sequin, 1 bead, 1 sequin, 1 bead and 1 sequin.
3. Sew these outwards from the centre bead a good 7.5 mm.
4. Bring the needle up at the opposite side of the bead and repeat, using the same amount of beads and sequins.
5. Make a third and fourth line at right angles to the first two.
6. Bring the needle back to the centre bead and make a looped petal between two straight lines by threading together 7 seed beads and sewing them to the centre.
7. Thread together 5 beads and sew between the two rows already sewn—this divides the beads to form a split beaded petal.

This flower is illustrated in Plate 4 inside the front cover.
The split beaded petal technique (Steps 6 and 7) is very useful for making leaves—I use it frequently for this purpose.

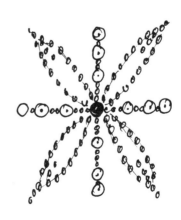

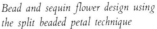

Bead and sequin flower design using the split beaded petal technique

Large sequinned flower

The large sequinned flower shown in Plate 4 inside the front cover is embroidered using a large sequin with a hole on the edge. This flower can only be formed with this particular sequin.

Method

1. Place a small square of interfacing on the back of a piece of fabric.
2. Using double thread, sew a large pearl or bead onto the material and interfacing, sewing twice through the pearl or bead to secure firmly.
3. Thread together on the needle: 1 sequin, 1 bead, 1 sequin, 1 bead and 1 sequin (3 sequins/2 beads) and pull them together, sewing outwards from the centre bead about 7.5 mm.

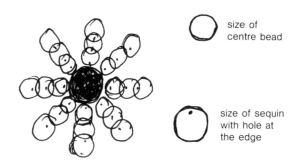

size of centre bead

size of sequin with hole at the edge

Sequin flower

4. Repeat this procedure 7 times so there are 8 rows surrounding the centre bead.

Each time you bring the needle back to the centre bead, sew a small stitch to hold the beads and sequins firm. The first sequin stands up around the centre of the bead and the last sequin lies flat on the material. This forms a pretty flower.

A spray based around the sequinned flower motif. This design has been greatly reduced in size—see the proportions of the flower at the top of the page

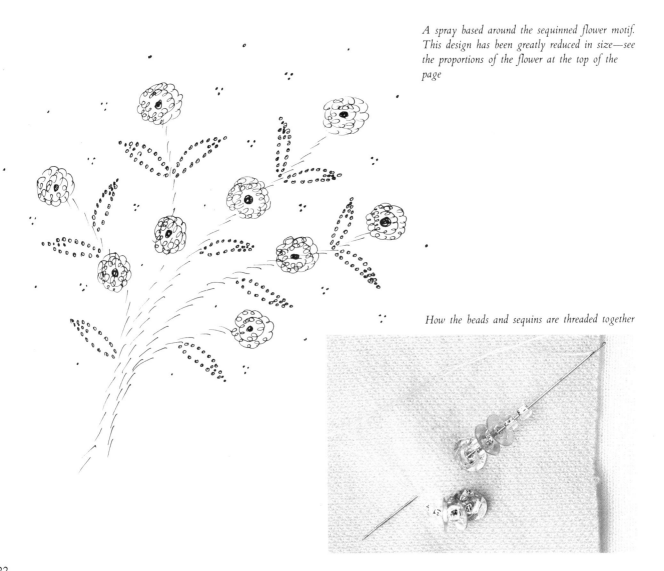

How the beads and sequins are threaded together

Small cup flower

You will need

1 small pearl
Chunky beads
Cup sequins

Method

1. Sew the centre pearl twice with double thread.
2. Thread 1 bead, 1 sequin, 1 bead and sew them out close to the central pearl.
3. Repeat Step 2 seven more times.

The sequins will stand to form a small cup flower. This is a good flower for filling in a design. It can also be incorporated into larger flower sprays. It appears in Plate 4 inside the front cover.

Large elaborate flower motif—enlarge to take up as much space as you want, or use as the basis for a multiple-flower design

Large flowers

You will need

1 large rhinestone
Size 3 bugle beads
Chunky beads
Sequins
Seed beads

Method

1. Trace the shape of the flower onto the garment.
2. With double thread, sew rhinestone in place for centre.
3. Sew a small bead over the hole of the rhinestone, bringing the needle through the stone and small bead and re-inserting it through the rhinestone. (This small bead covers the thread.)
4. Sew chunky beads around the edge of the stone, one at a time, picking up each bead with a whip stitch. Use as many as required to fit right around the rhinestone.

5. *Central flower:* Thread 3 seed beads, 1 sequin, 1 bead, 1 sequin, 1 bead and 1 sequin together and sew them about 7.5 mm outwards from a chunky bead.
6. Continue sewing around the stone from each chunky bead until the central flower is completed—this gives a raised look.
7. *Edge of flower:* Thread 3 seed beads together and sew from right to left around the outer edge of the flower. These beads should be angled.
8. Inside the edge, sew a row of angled bugle beads, one at a time.
9. The next row inside the bugle beads is sewn with 3 seed beads and 1 sequin. Sew by bringing the 3 beads from under the sequin. This gives the edge of the flower a three-dimensional look.
10. The inside of the flower can be beaded using a 'crazy' design. Sew each seed bead, one at a time, with a whip stitch, moving right to left. Clusters of 3 beads in a contrasting colour could be used inside the spaces of the 'crazy' design. See Plate 8 on page 17.

Sequin flowers

Complex design based on large sequinned flower, with leaves and scrolls added

You will need

Large bead or rhinestone
Chunky beads
Cup sequins
Small bead (seed)

Method

1. Draw the outlines of the design onto the fabric.
2. Sew a large rhinestone or bead for the centre of the flower, anchoring with a small seed bead.

3. Sew chunky beads, one at a time, around the outline of the flower.
4. Starting just inside the chunky bead outline, sew rows of cup sequins, one at a time, with whip stitches. Keep the sequins close so that very little thread shows.
5. Continue to sew rows of sequins around and around inside the flower until it is filled back to the centre.

Complex designs can be based on this type of flower, adding leaves and trailing scrolls, as illustrated above and in Plate 14.

This design can also be worked on the frame method (see pages 43–46).

Padded flowers

Padded bead-embroidered flowers can add sparkle and definition to a fancy cushion, or be used as a highlight on a dress. The flower should be taken from a good quality satin velvet or floral linen furnishing fabric—for example, the Sanderson's range of furnishing fabrics contains a large cabbage rose which is ideal for this type of work. Hibiscus are also suitable.

A fine iron-on padding now available is excellent for this type of work. Plate 16 shows unworked cabbage roses and an open-faced hibiscus; see Plate 35 on page 31 for examples of worked roses.

Method

1. Cut out the flowers and leaves required for your design.
2. Place them on the padding and iron according to the instructions. Trim.
3. Appliqué the padded flowers to the garment or cushion cover by machine or hand. The flower is then ready to embroider.
4. Follow the lines of the petal edges of the cabbage rose with seed beads, being careful to follow major crinkles and venation.

A lovely rhinestone with beads, sequins and pearls surrounding the stone could be used in a dangling arrangement in the centre of a hibiscus or other openfaced flower.

Australian flowers

A number of our Australian native flowers are good subjects for bead embroidery. I have not given specific instructions as you should be able to see from the photographs on page 29 how to approach each flower.

Waratah

The waratah can be embroidered in two ways—either appliquéd with red satin and beaded onto the garment (very dramatic on a dark background) or beaded in outline in red beads and sequins on a light background—Plates 25 and 26.

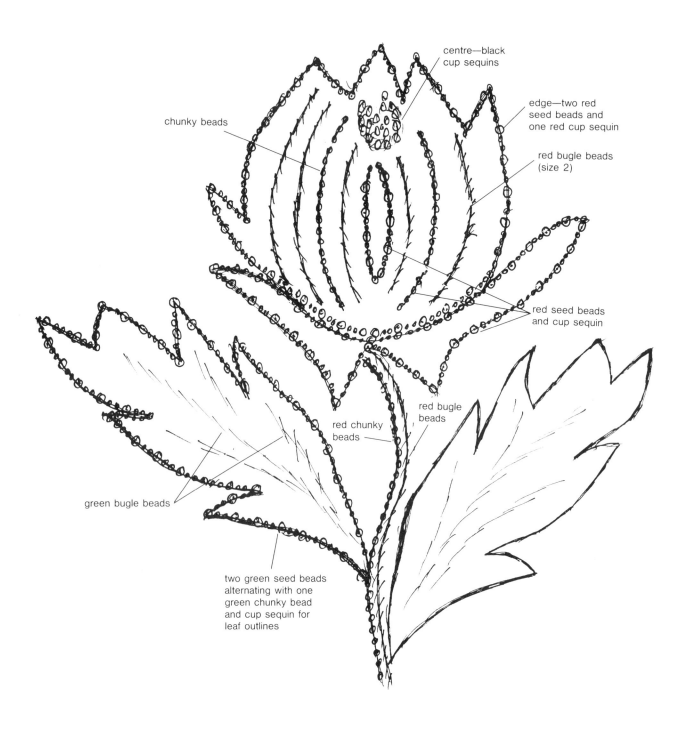

centre—black
cup sequins

edge—two red
seed beads and
one red cup sequin

chunky beads

red bugle beads
(size 2)

red seed beads
and cup sequin

red chunky
beads

red bugle
beads

green bugle beads

two green seed beads
alternating with one
green chunky bead
and cup sequin for
leaf outlines

Flannel flower

The flannel flower uses:
Mother-of-pearl sequins and satin white seed beads for the petals,
pale green sequins and pale green pearls for the centre.
Green bugle beads for the stems
Green seed beads for the leaves and the tips of the petals (Plate 24).

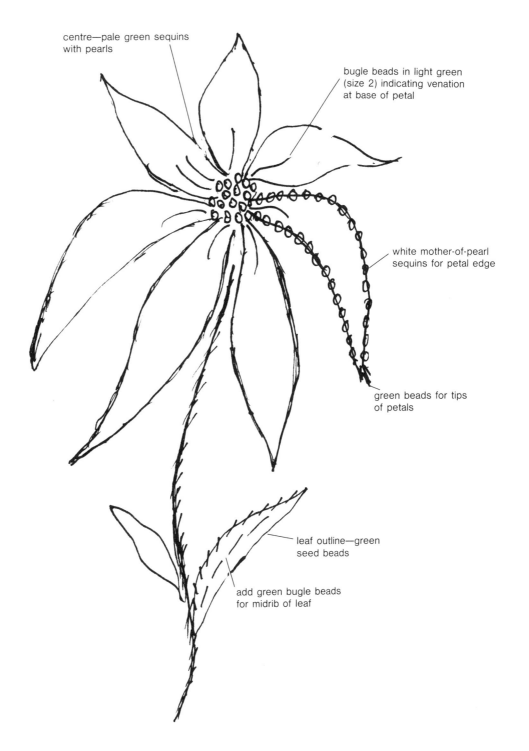

centre—pale green sequins with pearls

bugle beads in light green (size 2) indicating venation at base of petal

white mother-of-pearl sequins for petal edge

green beads for tips of petals

leaf outline—green seed beads

add green bugle beads for midrib of leaf

Gum blossom

Let your imagination run free with gum blossoms and gumnuts—but stay with these colours to start with!

Chocolate brown cup sequins for the base of the nut
Gold cup sequins for the top part of the flower
Gold chunky beads to outline the flower

Size 3 green bugle beads, green chunky beads and green sequins for the leaves
Red chunky beads for the top part of the flower spray

White or cream blossoms would also be effective on a dark background. See Plates 27 and 28, and page 33.

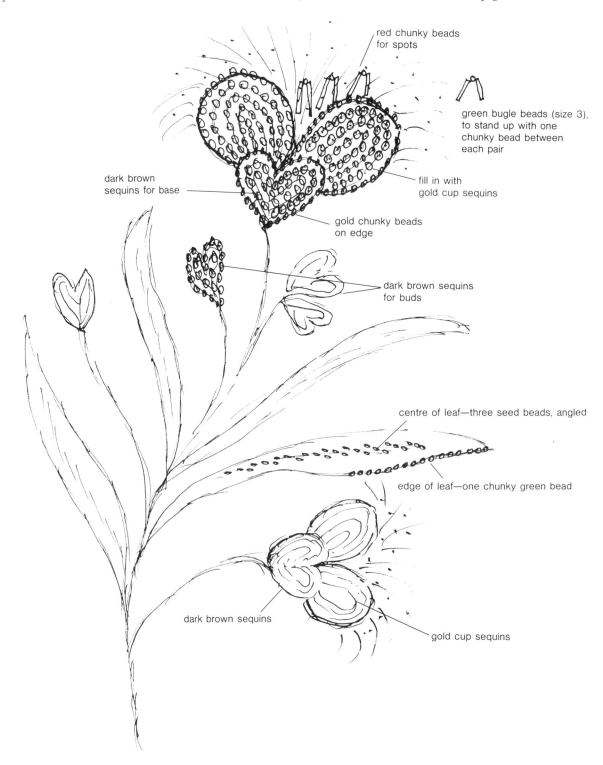

red chunky beads for spots

green bugle beads (size 3), to stand up with one chunky bead between each pair

dark brown sequins for base

fill in with gold cup sequins

gold chunky beads on edge

dark brown sequins for buds

centre of leaf—three seed beads, angled

edge of leaf—one chunky green bead

dark brown sequins

gold cup sequins

Australian flowers

Plate 24 *Flannel flower*

Plates 25 and 26 *Variations on the waratah*

Plates 27 and 28 *Variations on gum blossom*

Plate 29 *Wattle spray*

Plates 30 and 31 *Beaded evening bags and matching headbands (page 41)*

Plate 33 *A frame-beaded Peter Pan collar (page 46)*

Plate 32 *Modern crusted headbands covered in flowers*

Plate 34 *This large beaded collar, fashionable in the 1960s, was worked on a frame*

Plate 35 *A black evening top embroidered with padded flowers (page 25) trimmed with dangling arrangements in their centres. Spotting further enlarges the design*

31

Plate 36 *The scalloped neckline design in frame beading described on page 47*

Plate 37 *Heavily encrusted zig-zag beading worked on a frame (page 47)*

Plate 38 (left) *A black sheer crepe evening blouse which took a week to bead (page 46)*

Plate 39 (above) *Frame beaded evening bags in the style of the eighteenth century (page 46)*

Plate 40 (below) *Examples of the different types of beading that can be worked on a frame*

Wattle

The wattle spray has stems of green bugle beads with flowers formed of yellow sequins with a seed bead in the middle of each. See Plate 29.

green bugle beads
for stems

red chunky beads

green bugle beads

gold sequins

green seed beads
for leaves

flowers—one yellow
cup sequin with one
yellow seed bead

leaves—green seed
beads sewn in lines
angling from the stem

A variation of the gum blossom design

Scrolls with split leaf flowers

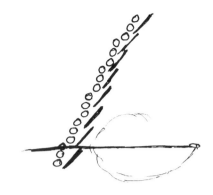

You will need

Seed beads
Size 2 bugle beads
Teardrops

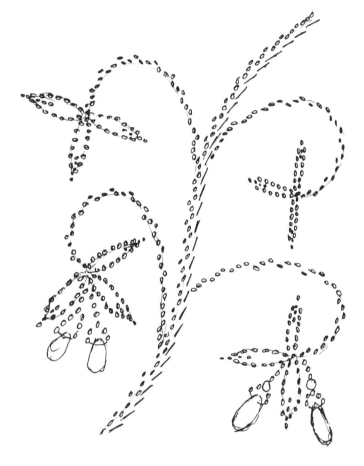

2. Thread a bugle bead and, working away from yourself but still sewing right to left, sew the bugle bead beside the 3 seed beds already sewn. This will form an opposite angle to that made by the seed beads and looks very pretty.

3. The outward scrolls are made up of a single line of 3 seed beads with a small half flower at the tip of each scroll made up of split leaves. With a pencil, mark three strokes—a centre and a further two strokes, one on each side of the centre.

4. Thread 6 seed beads and sew them out from the centre, ensuring they lie flat on the material. Finish this by sewing an additional stitch to hold firm.

5. With the needle, return to the beginning and thread a further 6 seed beads, sewing them from the stem.

6. Insert the needle between the two rows, thread up 4 beads and sew to the end of the two rows already sewn. This splits the section to form a petal.

7. Repeat this procedure until a half flower is embroidered on each end of the scroll. Sew the tear drops below the flowers to finish.

See Plate 10 on page 18.

This spray of scrolls and small half flowers can be enlarged, or added to, to make it a suitable size or shape for the area it is used in. Hanging teardrops are a glamorous addition to the flowers.

This design is beaded following a very simple method.

Method

1. After drawing the number of stems and scrolls required onto the garment, thread 3 seed beads and sew from right to left with a whip stitch. When sewn these beads angle downwards on the line.

This fancy scroll design uses chunky beads sewn one at a time, on a simple curve, with a whip stitch from right to left

Scrolls with sequin flowers

You will need

Seed beads
Chunky beads
Sequins
Large bead
Bugle beads

Method

This design can be enlarged if required.

1. Starting from the end of the right scroll, thread 3 seed beads and sew with a whip stitch, from right to left, working towards yourself.
2. Returning (working away from yourself), sew 1 chunky bead beside each group of 3 seed beads.
3. At the end of the scroll, add a half flower of seed beads and sequins—thread 3 seed beads, 1 sequin, 1 bead and 1 sequin—sew outwards from the centre bead.
4. Bring the needle back to the centre bead, beside the beads and sequins already sewn, and thread together 3 beads, 1 sequin, 1 bead, 1 sequin and sew outwards, beside the beads sewn.
5. Repeat this procedure until there are 5 petals sewn, forming a small half flower. Now sew a large bead to form the centre of the flower.
6. On the other section of the scroll, sew large bugle beads outwards from the stem, adding a chunky bead at the end of each bugle bead.

See Plate 11.

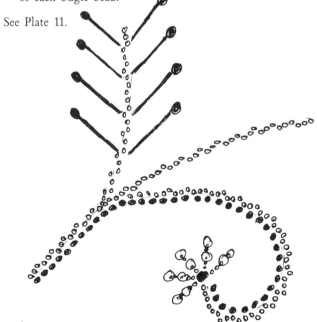

Fancy scrolls

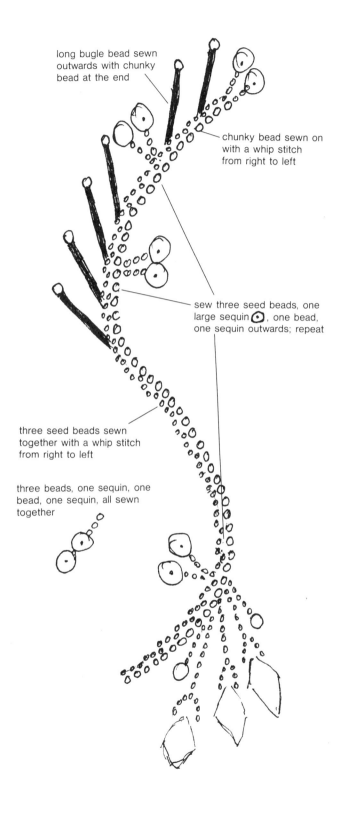

long bugle bead sewn outwards with chunky bead at the end

chunky bead sewn on with a whip stitch from right to left

sew three seed beads, one large sequin, one bead, one sequin outwards; repeat

three seed beads sewn together with a whip stitch from right to left

three beads, one sequin, one bead, one sequin, all sewn together

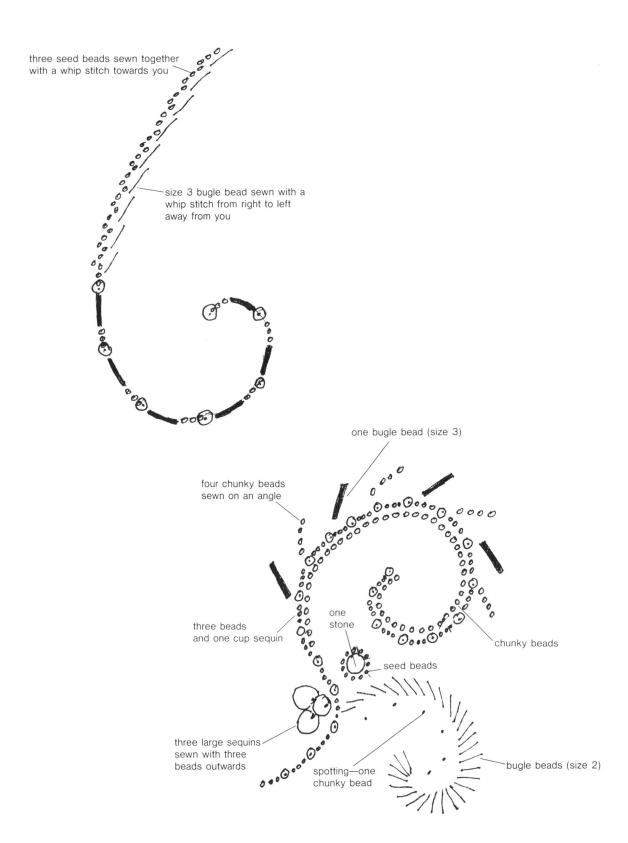

three seed beads sewn together
with a whip stitch towards you

size 3 bugle bead sewn with a
whip stitch from right to left
away from you

one bugle bead (size 3)

four chunky beads
sewn on an angle

chunky beads

three beads
and one cup sequin

one
stone

seed beads

three large sequins
sewn with three
beads outwards

spotting—one
chunky bead

bugle beads (size 2)

Diamond motif

You will need

Large oval shaped stone
Seed beads
Diamantes
Silver chunky beads
Teardrop pearls

Method

1. Sew the oval shaped stone onto material.
2. At the holes at each end of the stone sew a seed bead, inserting the needle back through the hole in the stone to secure to the material—this covers the original stitch.
3. Space 6 diamantes evenly to surround the central stone.
4. Sew two scalloped rows of silver chunky beads around the diamantes.
5. Sew a teardrop pearl between each scallop of the chunky beads. Remember to sew them in an outwards direction.
6. Add 1 teardrop to the lower part of the motif so that it hangs. To do this, thread 3 beads, the teardrop, and 3 more beads, sewing each side of the teardrop to form a hanging drop.

See Plate 12.

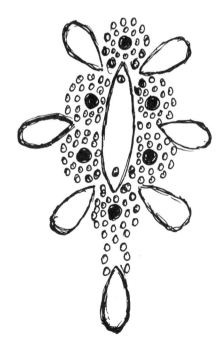

Dangling motif

You will need

Round rhinestone
Seed beads
9 large pearls
Silver chunky beads
1 teardrop pearl with hole through centre

Method

1. Sew the round rhinestone onto the material.
2. At the holes on each side of the stone, sew a seed bead, inserting the needle back through the hole in the stone to secure it to the material. This covers the original stitch.
3. Space 6 large pearls evenly to surround the central stone.
4. Sew 1 scalloped row of silver chunky beads around the large pearls.
5. Add 1 teardrop to the lower part of the motif so that it hangs. To do this, thread 3 seed beads, 1 large pearl, 1 bead and 1 teardrop through the centre, with 1 bead on the end of the teardrop, to form the hanging drop.
6. Insert the needle back through the teardrop, pearl and seed beads, leaving the end bead to anchor the drop, pearl and beads.
7. On each side of this hanging drop, sew 10 seed beads with 1 large pearl and 1 seed bead on the end. Insert the needle back through these beads to hang each side of the centre hanging drop.

See Plate 12.

Techniques

Spotting

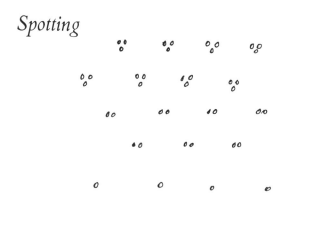

Spotting is quite often used to make a design look larger. It also fills in spaces where it would not be possible to extend the design. Spotting is clusters of 3 seed beads sewn individually in a 3, 2, 1, formation.

Cluster centre

You will need

Large bead for centre
Bugle beads
Sequins
Seed beads

Method

1. Sew the centre bead of the flower, twice, to hold firm.
2. Thread together and sew 1 bugle bead, 1 sequin and 1 seed bead, inserting the needle back through the sequin and bugle bead, and using a whip stitch to anchor them.

bugle bead (size 3)

centre bead

sequin with bead
in the centre

This arrangement stands up and can be repeated as many times as required to form a centre.

Zig-zag

You will need

Size 3 bugle beads
Seed beads
Sequins

Method

1. Sew the bugle beads in a zig-zag fashion along a curve or scroll.
2. Inside each V of the beads thread together 3 seed beads, 1 sequin, 1 seed bead, 1 sequin and sew outwards from the centre of the V.

See Plate 13.

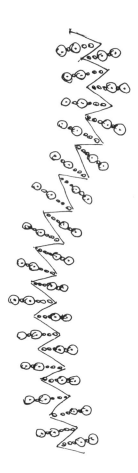

Dangling arrangements

You will need

Seed beads
Cup sequins

Method

1. Working from the appliquéd edge of a padded flower thread together 3 beads, 1 cup sequin (cup side up), 1 bead, 1 cup sequin.
2. Sew these outwards on the edge, bringing the needle back through beside the 3 beads.
3. Sew beads and sequins in this manner around the edge, keeping the spacing very even.

Stamens could also be added to the flower, or other dangling arrangements in the centre. This is the method used on the padded flower in Plate 35.

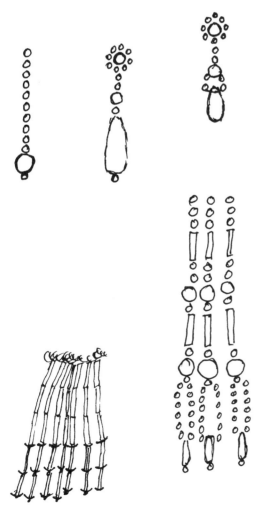

Single fringing

This style of single fringing is also called Cleopatra fringing. It can be used to decorate a garment in various places.

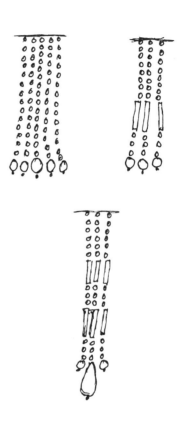

You will need

Seed beads
Teardrop pearl with a hole through the centre

Method

1. Thread together 12 seed beads, 1 teardrop and 1 seed bead.
2. Insert the needle back through the teardrop and beads, leaving the seed bead on the end to anchor the string of beads.
3. Continue in this manner, using more or less beads, depending on the length of the fringing required.
4. Bugle beads can replace a number of seed beads for variety; various sizes of teardrops can be used; even chunky beads.

Single looped fringing

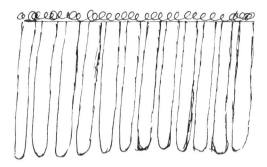

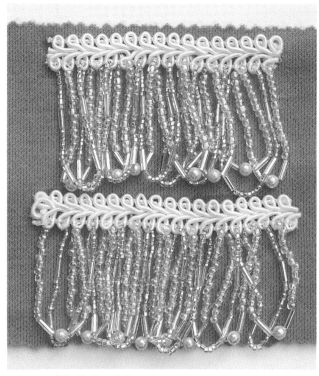

Method

1. Thread approximately 40 seed beads (vary the number for the length required).
2. Loop this string of beads and sew onto the material close to the starting point, but not so close that the line of beads buckles.
3. Continue sewing loops along an edge or where required.

Vary the beads on the loop by using bugle beads amongst the seed beads.

Two rows of double looped fancy fringing hanging from a braid edge

Double looped fringing

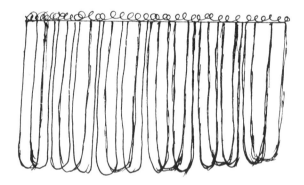

Double looped fringing follows the same principles as single looped fringing; however, when bringing the threaded beads back to the material, leave a good 3 mm space between the stitches, as you have to return to the centre of this space with the second loop to make the double looped fring.

Bugle beads, or a combination of bugle beads and pearls, can be used.

Plates 20 and 21 illustrate double looped beaded fringing and a pretty lampshade. Sequins and beads can be added as further trimming. Double looped fringing can be incorporated into a design to decorate almost any part of a garment.

Fancy fringing

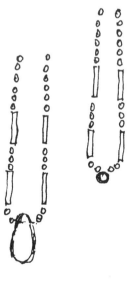

These diagrams show just two of the many possible variations of looped fringing. The only constraint is the size of the beads—too large a bead will spoil the 'flow' of the fringe.

Advanced designs

Embroidered snake

The embroidered snake shown in Plate 23 is heavily encrusted with seed, chunky and bugle beads, together with sequins. A few rhinestones have also been included. This elaborate piece of work combines all the flatwork methods shown in this book. All gold beads used are 9 carat gold lined.

Evening bags and headbands

Plates 30 and 31 show evening bags beaded in the 1950s with 9 carat gold lined beads, seed pearl beads and black beads. The matching jewelled headbands were embroidered between 1980 and 1990. They are made up from wide plastic headbands covered with padding and fabric, embroidered with rhinestone drops, beads and gold and mother-of-pearl sequins. All the bags were beaded by the frame method. The working time was two days for each bag—see page 46.

Dolls

Dolls' garments can be embroidered with beads, sequins and pearls. Plate 19 shows a collection of little dolls with beaded gowns—too special to play with, but entertaining to work on.

Fine lace

Fine lace is a joy to embroider as you can embroider the pattern onto the lace with tiny beads, delicate sequins and small stones, adding all kinds of decorations to the lace. The border of the lace can also be outlined with beads, etc. The doll shown in Plate 22 is dressed with a gown of delicate lace. The gown is a copy of an adult gown.

Chantilly and guipure lace can look very elegant embroidered with beads and sequins.

Chantilly lace is soft and can be delicately beaded and sequinned. Brides look magnificent in Chantilly gowns encrusted at the neckline, bodice and hem with pearls and crystals.

Guipure lace is much heavier. Guipure lace flowers can be cut out and beaded and made into many designs on linen or other heavy materials. Chalk beads are particularly suitable for this type of work; they can be used for stems, with other beads and drops to decorate the design—see Plate 17.

The sketch shows a design with guipure lace flowers.

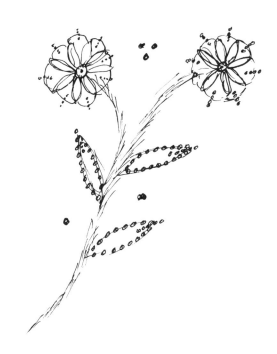

Guipure lace flowers

You will need

Size 3 bugle beads in chalk or satin (for flower stems)
Seed beads (for flowers and leaves)
Large beads (for flower centres)

Method

1. From the lace cut out flowers to make up a beading design.
2. Place the flowers in position on the fabric to make up a spray.
3. With a fade-away pencil, draw lines between the flowers for the stems and leaves.

4. Sew a large bead through the flower centre, together with a small coloured seed bead as an anchor.

5. Fasten the tip of each flower petal with 4 seed beads, sewn together. Follow with an additional small stitch to hold firm.

6. The stems of the spray are beaded with size 3 bugle beads one at a time on an angle. Start the stem by sewing the first bugle bead the length of the bead away from the flower onto the drawn line, angled, with a back stitch.

7. Start the next bugle halfway along the first bead, again at an angle.

8. Continue down the line in this manner.

9. For the leaves, thread 8 seed beads together and sew outwards from the stem, laying them flat on the material and anchoring with a small stitch.

10. Thread another 8 seed beads and sew these back to the stem, securing with a small stitch.

11. Take the needle under the fabric between the lines of beads, bringing it up about 3 beads from the outer end, and thread a further 5 seed beads.

12. Sew these in the same manner, splitting the two rows to form the leaf.

Study Plate 17 on page 19 for guidance if you are confused. If you wish, add some cluster spotting to the spray, using 3 large beads (the same size as the centre of the flower), and 3 coloured seed beads (to top the large central beads).

1. Sew the 3 large beads individually to form a cluster.
2. Anchor a coloured seed bead to the top of each large bead, inserting the needle back through each large bead to secure it to the cluster.

Tie-shaped collar

The collar illustrated in the frontispiece (page 2) was beaded on linen with chalk beads and 'shot' navy seed beads; bugle beads, and larger beads for the centres, were added. Seven chalk seed beads were threaded together and stitched down to form the looped scalloped edge finish.

Sweaters (illustrated insde the back cover)

Plum coloured sweater

Plate 41 shows a plum-coloured double knitted sweater with velvet padded flower heavily embroidered. The flower is enhanced with leaves and scrolls; amethyst beads and sequins blend in with the plum colour.

A silver rhinestone, together with silver rosemonties and outlines of silver beads, has been added.

Aqua sweater

Plate 42 illustrates an aqua-coloured double knitted top, heavily embroidered with sequinned flowers and scrolls. This design combines many of the methods shown earlier in the book.

Jade green pure wool jumper

Cream lace flowers have been appliquéd to make the design shown in Plate 43. Loops and scrolls trail to connect the lace flowers. Use jade seed beads, 9 carat gold lined beads, rhinestones and pearls to decorate the lace flowers.

A rhinestone-cut flower is added to the centre, surrounded with the cup flower of sequins. Tiny gold beads are finally looped around the cup flower to finish the centre.

Cut jade drops form the hanging arrangements.

White sweater

The cotton/polyester sweater shown in Plate 44 features a paisley design. Paisley designs can vary as much as scroll designs, and can be taken from any paisley designed fabric.

Wattle embroidered jumper

A spray of wattle embroidered onto a fluffy wool jumper (Plate 45) looks very pretty. See page 33 for instructions on how to bead this particular spray.

Navy blue sweater

This sweater has been embroidered with a contrasting suede leather flower appliquéed, which has then been beaded and sequinned around the edge. Scrolls made up of wooden beads, copper-shot bugle beads and seed beads, together with a few black beads, are added. Large black sequins are also sewn to form a couple of flowers.

The centre is a dangling arrangement made from large natural wooden beads. See Plate 46.

Black evening top

The black jersey knitted top shown in Plate 35 on page 31 uses a Sanderson's furnishing fabric cabbage rose design. The flowers are cut out and appliquéed to the sweater. On this particular garment I have used pink roses embroidered with amethyst beads, gun metal sequins, large silver rhinestones, silver beads and small silver rosemonties, outlined with silver beads. The hanging arrangements dangling from the centres of the roses are made up of pink pearls, teardrops and black beads.

French frame beading

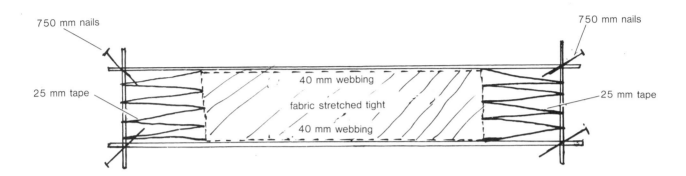

750 mm nails

750 mm nails

25 mm tape

25 mm tape

40 mm webbing

fabric stretched tight

40 mm webbing

Frame for French frame beading

French frame beading is very different to hand beading. It is much more difficult to learn but is definitely a quicker method when working a large design onto a garment. It requires a rectangular timber frame made up from dressed oregon or a similar timber, measuring:

    2 lengths of 1370 mm × 50 mm × 50 mm

    2 lengths of 710 mm × 30 mm × 20 mm

    2 × 750 mm nails

    40 mm webbing

The two 1370 mm lengths require a rectangular slot or hole cut through each end, approximately 10–15 mm from the ends; to allow the two 710 mm lengths to be passed through. The 710 mm lengths need to have staggered holes equidistant from each end, large enough for a 150 mm nail to pass through easily (easily visible in Plate 00). The 1370 mm lengths and the 150 mm nails are used to fasten the frame together. Pass the 710 mm lengths through the rectangular slots of the 1370 mm pieces. A length of 40 mm webbing, approximately 1100 mm,

is tacked in position along one side of each longer length of wood. The material to be beaded is pinned to the webbing on each side, being stretched very tight from one side of the frame. The nails are inserted when the required tension is achieved.

Let's say the garment to be beaded is a bodice. The shape of the bodice is traced onto the fabric. The design to be worked is then drawn on the wrong side of the material, the material is pinned to the webbing on the frame, stretched very tight and secured with the nails. The other edges of the fabric are pinned to lengths of 25 mm wide tape wound around the end timbers of the frame. (See the photograph on the next page, and the drawing.)

The frame is now set up for the first stage of French frame beading, which is worked with a cornaly needle fitted into a needle holder made from an old-type wooden pen handle, or something similar, approximately 150 mm in overall length. An instrument maker or jeweller could make needle holders (see illustration) with little trouble.

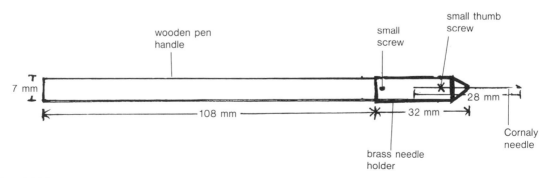

wooden pen handle

small thumb screw

small screw

7 mm

108 mm

32 mm

28 mm

brass needle holder

Cornaly needle

Cornaly needle and holder

Method

Take a spool of machine thread the same colour as the material to be beaded; pass a strand of beads onto the thread by tying the thread from the strand of beads and the thread. The beads are passed on, together with a small slip knot.

Holding the thread in the left hand under the frame and the needle holder in the right hand, insert the needle into the material and pick up the thread between your thumb and forefinger to form a chain stitch. The chain stitch is worked to the size of the beads you will be using. Sequins are threaded wrong side on to the thread so they are right side up when finished.

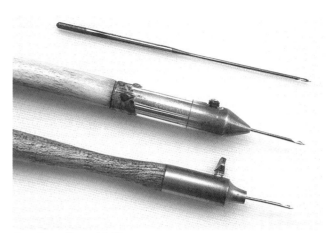

Cornaly needles and holders

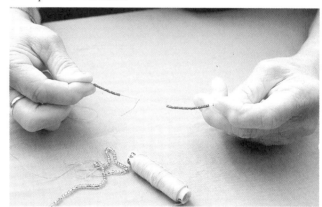

Threading the beads

Making a stitch

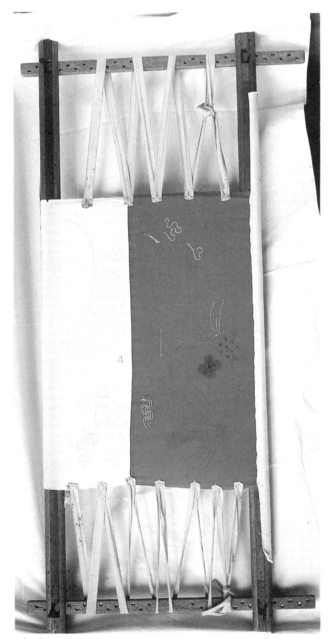

The frame set up for use

How to hold the needle

A sleeveless top fully beaded with a 'crazy' pattern, a border of beads around neck and armholes, and even a fringe to finish

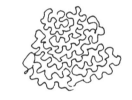

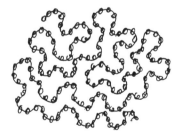

Close beading can be used to fill in sections of the 'crazy' design

beads

sequins

Starburst pattern using alternate bead and sequin rays

Embroidered blouse

The black sheer crepe blouse is beaded with gunmetal beads and sequins. It took me a week to bead it.

The design is made up of broken straight lines radiating from the neck downwards. Every fifth line was interrupted with size 2 bugle beads.

In between these lines are broken lines of seed beads. I hand beaded between the breaks with three seed beads and a sequin to give a sunray effect.

All the seams are hand sewn from the shoulder so as not to disturb the beads. The neck facing was sewn on by hand with sequins and beads to finish the neckline.

Collars

Peter Pan collar

The collar shown in Plate 33 was frame beaded in linen with chalk and wooden beads, with bugle beads being added to make the designs.

Large collar

The frame beaded collar in Plate 34 is used to fit a square necked shirt or dress, with a drop over the shoulder forming a V at the back. Blue and white bugle beads, together with chalk beads, were used. The collar has a looped scalloped edge to finish.

This type of beading was very fashionable in the 1960s.

Lines of seed beads, sequins and bugle beads radiate from the neckline of this sheer crepe blouse

Vintage evening bags

The evening bags in Plate 39 in are the style used in the eighteenth century. They were embroidered using the French frame method. I then stitched the sides together by hand and lined the bags with pure silk. A fancy fringe finishes the lower edge of the bags.

Three-cut seed beads were used for the main part of the beading. All gold beads used were 9 carat gold lined.

Crusted frame beading

Heavily encrusted beading was very fashionable in the 1960s. This type of beading can be embroidered on a frame using a cornaly needle and chain stitch.

The design is traced onto the wrong side of the garment to be beaded and the beading is worked from the wrong side of the garment, which is attached to the frame.

Working with the cornaly needle, make a chain stitch by moving 4 beads (threaded together) to the material. Insert the cornaly needle again to make another chain stitch which will anchor the 4 beads. The length of the chain stitch should allow the 4 beads to be raised slightly (in a small loop fashion) from the fabric.

Working in a zig-zag manner will give the heavily crusted effect shown in Plate 37.

Design for a neckline

You will need

Seed beads
Size 2 bugle beads

This particular design is suitable for use around the neck of a garment.

Method

1. Draw two shaped lines around the neckline approximately 2.5 cm apart. From these lines draw an equal number of half scallops to fit each line as shown in the diagram. (The size of the scallops and the width between the lines are matters of personal choice.)
2. The straight lines are beaded with seed beads. Along the scalloped lines are size 2 bugle beads. To give the crusty look count out 6 seed beads, crossing them over the bugle beads in a looped fashion to form a zig-zag from one side to the other.
3. If you wish, drops or loops of beads can hang from the scallops.

This design can be worked on the frame or beaded with the hand method. See Plate 36.

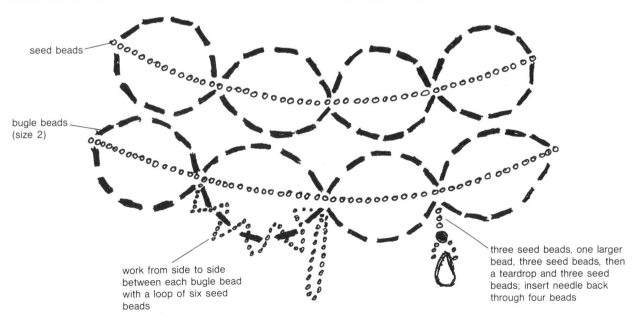

seed beads

bugle beads
(size 2)

work from side to side between each bugle bead with a loop of six seed beads

three seed beads, one larger bead, three seed beads, then a teardrop and three seed beads; insert needle back through four beads

Suppliers

All the beads, sequins, pearls and trimmings shown in this book can be purchased from:

Photios Bros Pty Limited
66 Druitt Street
Sydney NSW 2000
(02) 267 1428

Comprehensive ranges of beads and findings are also carried by:

Bead Co. of Australia*
497 Elizabeth Street
Surry Hills 2010
(02) 318 2775

Beads Galore Pty Ltd
25a Playfair Street
The Rocks, Sydney 2000
(02) 247 5946

Beadz of Hurstville
324 Forest Road
Hurstville 2220
(02) 580 4923

We've Got The Beads
577 Elizabeth Street
Redfern NSW 2016
(02) 319 3355

Stadia Handcrafts
85 Elizabeth Street
Paddington 2021
(02) 328 7900

The Bead Co. of Victoria*
336 Smith Street
Collingwood 3066
(03) 419 0636

Maria George Pty Ltd
179 Flinders Lane
Melbourne 3000
(03) 650 1151
(03) 650 4117

Glamour 'N' Glitter Pty Ltd
49 Atkinson Street
Chadstone 3148
(03) 563 1300

Bead & Trimming Co.*
69 Elizabeth Street
Brisbane 4000
(07) 221 1315

The Bead Shop*
190 Goodwood Road
Millswood 5034
(08) 373 1296

Tanami Garden Centre
Paterson Street
Tennant Creek 0860
(089) 62 2809

*indicates mail order service available.

Many department stores and haberdashers also carry a range of beads.